A POST CARD TO

a Post Card to

JOHN GREENING & STUART HENSON

RED SQUIRREL PRESS

First published in 2021 by Red Squirrel Press
36 Elphinstone Crescent
Biggar
South Lanarkshire
ML12 6GU
www.redsquirrelpress.com

Typeset and designed by Gerry Cambridge
 e: gerrycambridge@btinternet.com

A CIP catalogue record for this book is available from The British Library.

ISBN: 978 1 913632 02 1

Red Squirrel Press is committed to a sustainable future. This book is printed
in the UK by Imprint Digital using Forest Stewardship Council certified paper.
www.digital.imprint.co.uk

'What? my friend!
A sonnet?'

—*Walter Savage Landor*

a Post Card to

Preface

There is a long tradition of exchanges between poets, very often in the form of an 'epistle'. Between such (generally lengthy) verse correspondence and today's smartphone 'poetweets' there was, for a century or so, the picture postcard – and its lankier cousin, the letter-card. They are becoming harder to find even in tourist spots these days, but a certain generation would feel that their holiday was incomplete if they hadn't bought a card and a stamp, written a few clichés in ballpoint, and then wondered where on earth they could find a postbox. As friends born in the same year, Stuart and I liked to exchange cards, but we felt that the available space demanded something more than the usual platitudes. It was also roughly sonnet-shaped...   JG

Believe it or not, sonnets actually do fit on postcards. It has to be done with what Michael Schmidt describes as 'excellent economy'. The secret is to rough it out on a sheet of paper or in a notebook – and then write *small*. We've tried to avoid making it an obligation (hence the long gaps between), but over the years the form has served to capture some far-flung thoughts. Putting the selection together has been a bit like riffling through forgotten snapshots from the backs of drawers, and I'm more than grateful to John for preserving so many of mine that might otherwise have disappeared into the dead-letter box of history.   SH

Contents

A Postcard to Stuart Henson

Dear Stuart: rain's still streaming down the glass,
and once again we've not been able to get out...
A day at the dinner table then, door shut,
Grandma asleep. Blue willow-pattern vases,
blue willow-pattern plates. Time passes
and nothing is on the page. I begin to doubt
my own abilities – but one can't spout
poetry like rain, you'd tell me. One must cast
gently into the stream, into that blue, fast-
flowing moment when the mind is in spate;
lean quietly on the Chinese bridge; and wait
for the line to quiver, the reel to at last
unwind, wrestling with – unable to see –
this silvery form, a sonnet (from JDG).

JG to SH from Frome, Somerset, 1985

A Postcard to John Greening

The long, empty perspective of the beach
at dusk, the tide-line ragged, the odd gull
mewing alone, far out across the reaches
of silt that merge invisibly with the swell;
the green salt smell of the pools, the oily
detritus and the tell-tale tracks of man
and boy – all that accumulates, slowly,
washed up on the mind's receptive strand;
these are our keepsakes, wispy souvenirs
for the year inland where time is hard-edged
and the wind forgets its promises: the clear
uncomplicated days our childhoods pledged –
to wanderers with nets and spades who planned
great bridges, ships and mansions in the sand.

SH to JG from North Norfolk, 1989

With Ruth

She walks us down the road to Brooklyn Heights,
the loaded summer air on its last fling,
where children roll in gold sand, slide and swing
towards the fairy far Manhattan lights.
Here Gentile races Jew, Blacks climb with Whites,
and no one fears that sudden violent spring
round a cold corner. Here New Yorkers string
fluorescent dreams about their day, these sights
she's brought us out to see – a glitzy frieze
with bright-eyed kids. But where her own eyes rest,
darknesses start moving in a grid pattern
to cross a darker river, shadows seize
brightness by the strap, stab a star-pocked breast –
and won't be smiled out, not by all Manhattan.

JG to SH from Clinton, NJ, 1990

a Post Card to

(untitled)

Another postcard, a salutation,
bright but unlooked for, like the sudden plume
of vapour from the steel-works at Margam
picked out by sunlight. No explanation.
It's there, and then a gradual dissipation
into air and cloud – a puff of white steam,
a genie, deceptive as all that gleams
at a distance – an odd fascination.
As I sit down to write it haunts the view
across this little stretch of boat-bobbed sea
well cursed and versed by Thomas in his day,
and doubtless quite familiar to you –
old student of the university
of lights and tides that wash round Swansea Bay.

SH to JG from the Mumbles, 1993

a Post Card to

(untitled)

Landscape of mists, of fortresses and falls
where Edward's thirteenth-century castles rise
out of the native rock, and Turner skies
wash in like tides against their crumbling walls.
The old campaigners in their feasting halls
knew well enough how much they were despised,
how time already worked at their demise
and every glade seethed Glyndwr's rallying-calls.
Here, Wales and England wrote their ties in blood
and parcelled ancient kingdoms into shires.
Two languages that claim the ground as theirs:
a cloven heritage that Johnson trod.
Where R.S.Thomas coughs his bitter Airs
and Hopkins gushed his sad-glad songs to God.

SH to JG from North Wales, 1994

a Post Card to

Rhine Journey

The middle stretch is difficult, but I
have kept returning to that long ripe curve
and found it navigable, buoy-marked, safe
for any scribbling Siegfried to get by –
to blow his horn and set out heroically
each day. The middle-aged poet's groove
has dated, while Hildegard, rejuvenated,
sings hologram duets with Lorelei.
The vineyards on the terraces are locked
like monkish books, bound in their cells, loaded
with chants and *Minnelieder* and boredom.
The middle stretch has two sides: one of them –
unless you are a heroine encoded
in a fashionable ring of fire – neglect.

JG to SH from Bingen, 1995

a Post Card to

To Johannes Gutenberg

You taught us how the world could be contained
between stiff boards, reduced to type, to a row
of lead: preserved, passed on by mirror-code
to any future, even this, where multi-laned
our information runs its rings, hare-brained,
and wails and mocks the passing of the slow
cold dawn of print on page. Books will still grow
as grapes are red. But look – this untrained
circuitry is cocooning us: no need
for labour here, the hourly vintage plays
direct from every lap, its icons bubble
a character from light with lightning speed
and disregard for all you hauled, screwed, pressed
out of the dark – yes, and thought immovable.

JG to SH from Mainz, 1995

a Post Card to

A Yew Tree

Lady Anne Clifford speaks:

'We have looked inward for generations,
sure of the right to power. At our command
the stone was brought, the battle fought, the land
put to the plough. The brute population
born into service, ranked by their stations,
fell foul at Flodden, loyal to a man.
But then a different world to understand:
our walls slighted to the foundations.
Well, I had Cromwell's lease to build again
though I must tolerate his rabble troop
tramping my conduit court and not ask why.
And now in the Year of Our Lord 1659
I plant this yew, to grow like a green hope
in a waste place, spreading towards the sky.'

SH to JG from Skipton Castle, 1995

a Post Card to

Rievaulx

With Nature green and greedy all about,
the eminent Victorians thought of her
halfway between a goddess and a whore:
as something they could worship and exploit.
Romantically, they languished to be taught
the lessons of her lovely landscapes where
their mighty hearts stood still, their spirits soared,
and minds worked out how cheaply she'd be bought.

A noble ruin dignified a scene:
maybe an abbey by a waterfall.
The quarry owner's mansion in the dale
stood righteous on that abbey's stolen stone.
The railway huffed and puffed around the fell,
as if its smoky incense might atone.

SH to JG from Rievaulx Abbey, Yorkshire, 1997

a Post Card to

At Auvers-sur-Oise

In cornfields where no crows but only larks
dab invisibly at the grey, visualise
him clipped, folded, carried out of church to skies
he made immortal; feel the earth relax
into a catalogue of squares to harvest,
yields that press for higher prices; follow this lane
where traffic leaves the ear unsavaged; open
the gates, pass through, and find the brothers' graves,
Theo, Vincent, bonded with ivy leaves
from Dr Gachet's garden, the connoisseur
who tended that small plot where there would rise
seventy suns, and one unfissionable life
sink down, for fear of crows and corn, for fear
of supernovae at Auvers-sur-Oise.

JG to SH from France, 1998

a Post Card to

(untitled)

The First People were not the first: always
there were others before them – the hopeful,
the brave, the foolhardy and the cruel,
all of them looking west, searching the skies
for smoke, a portent, the sign that a day's
journey would bring them at last the rich soil,
the ground where the spread seed would never fail;
somewhere to prosper and grow old and wise.

A man could lose his past, make a new world
and build a home to raise good daughters in,
or better still, good sons: a land of gold
and grass in the sunset. You bought a gun,
a trap, a lamp for the long nights, a rolled
blanket, and five bushels of the best grain.

SH to JG from Winnipeg, 2000

a Post Card to

Ouroboros

Some islands are no more than those we see
on summer evenings – clouds beyond the glass
that shape archipelagos of light, and gloss
our storm-beaten dreams. Others feel wintry
and real – have motorbikes, are sanctuary
to dogma, gull, anthrax; a royal house;
Thelwell's ponies; or Muir's heraldic horse...
Though John Donne rings in our ears at the ferry
and bridge, tolling the mainland, still our need
for solitude keeps pressing here where crowds
are pasted up against shopfronts while cars
tourney and quest for space. The errant creed
is 'we move on'. But on islands, all roads
return to meet themselves, their one route ours.

JG to SH from Camelford, North Cornwall, 2000

a Post Card to

Akureyri, 5 a.m.

I'm almost on the Arctic Circle here
in Akureyri, where a polar chill
nips at the day-long sun and there is still
white streaking the sides of the fjord, sheer,
sharp-toothed in its smiling. The light's as clear
as Icelandic water, a light that will
go on and on the way life seems to until
you reach a point... Is that an alarm I hear?
My father, waking from the winter dark
in nineteen forty-three, notes with delight
the first birdsong to have dawned on him in three
long months of blackout. Sparrow, starling, arctic
tern or golden plover? Whatever, the night
is over and the long day faces me.

JG to SH from Iceland, 2001

[25]

a Post Card to

From Edinburgh
(with portrait of Hugh MacDiarmid)

Hail from the land beyond the savage wall
(more civil and more cultured than the south)
where talent can be blessed with word-of-mouth
success and every August many are called
to strut and fret their hour; where every room's
a stage and all the men and women seem
to be comedians and siren dreams
of stardom lure fools to financial doom.

The Festival! The Fringe! Democracy
gone mad: the thrice-three-muses bacchanal
where everyone – sublime, bizarre, banal –
has more than fifteen minutes'-worth of fame.
What will survive? Only the poetry.
Here's mad MacDiarmid/Grieve. (What's in a name?)

SH to JG from Edinburgh, 2005

a Post Card to

Deaths in Venice
(a lettercard)

I

A horn call over the lagoon: he's dead,
the carnival's masked hero, darkest knight
in all its glittering shallows. Wagner's deathbed
accompaniment – his 'Farewell' – was a bright
and cheerful *gondolieri* tune. His head
dropped forward, pocket watch slipped out of sight
and stopped, the grail is lost and music floats
to its funeral. Twelve oars. A row of notes.

a Post Card to

II

Another blast. Another slow cortège
from *Ca' Rezzonico* now, the home of Pen
whose ink has run so low his father's page
is blank, for all those years of love and lend.
Fame throws its rope towards the landing stage
and misses, falls into the bluey green
oblivion of the Grand Canal, as Robert Browning
departs and leaves his dry son drowning.

a Post Card to

III

Dim land. Peace. Then a brassy broadcast sound
between the gondolas; invisible waves
breaking over stages, unsettling ground
whose very foundations rot. Literature heaves
its driftwood, bringing with it Ezra Pound
to cemetery island. A storm raves
and seaweed scribbles free verse in the sand;
the Lido goes on listening to its oompah band.

IV

No sound when they lay down Diaghilev
or when Stravinsky joined him for that one
last dance through time, beyond belief
and into myth. Watched by the evening sun
behind the city, from their spotlit grave
they count the dreadful complex beats that soon
will tell them: your scene's over. But the rite
they share this time is one long opening night.

JG to SH from Venice, 2007

a Post Card to

Pageant of the Golden Tree

To watch some seventy floats come rolling by
is role reversal. Not the world observing
another year of your existence curving
to the square. Not you on stilts, or mounted high
in potent armour, following a sigh
from pasteboard towers. Not you this time: chained, serving
a prince, or playing the serpent, or deserving
brief flickering applause at the crowd's eye.
Time stops instead to watch these mannerists
who span the city with an allegory
such lives as mine must sit through to discover
how one cart plays its heart out while one rests,
how war-drums turn to jingled revelry,
how each scene wipes the next until it's over.

JG to SH from Bruges, 2007

a Post Card to

In the John Rylands Library

'A fair day's wages for a fair day's work'
was what they asked, the Ancoats Brotherhood.
You hear their voices still, half choked with soot
and drifting heavenward like the city's smoke
while in the library the altered air
of knowledge filters round the hide-bound texts.
Philanthropy in this world. For the next,
printed indulgences, Bibles, culture
in all its variants. Is Rylands' coin
enough to buy his place among the saints?
He paid the going rate: they've no complaints.
A devil coughs and coughs and coughs again.
  A fair day's hire. Define it if you can.
  'Half what you'd have to pay a gentleman'.

SH to JG from Manchester, 2009

a Post Card to

To my Friend Stuart Henson Esquire

Michael Drayton speaks:

'While we can hear, our works still get a mention –
so long as poets read, speak, show some taste,
they're wanted. Then they start to crave attention
and nail their desperate writings to the mast
as *HMS Remembrance of Things Past*
begins to sink. This, then, is my Idea:
we make all poets pass a writing test
on reaching a set age. If they've a Lear
like Will's in them, if Senex proves his best
is still to come, then we grant licences
with key restrictions, such as *may not rest*
on laurels or start sonnet sequences
or any verses which – even if they ask
in bended metres – might be used for masque.'

JG to SH from Hawthornden Castle, West Lothian, 2010

[33]

Hardyesque

Low voices, a knocking, from the chantry:
time past and present in conversation.
Slowly the labour of conservation
drip-feeds the tomb-sleep of antiquity.
Recumbent lords re-cast in alabaster –
an anaesthetic dream they never woke from
lulled by the long assurance of unbroken
patronage, each in his place, the master
and the peasant at his gate, their property
a token of their share in God's estate.
Noseless and eyeless now they are betrayed;
their dates have faded into history.
Carved in the gallery a bold TH
asserts its counter-claim for immortality.

SH to JG from Puddletown, Dorset, 2010

a Post Card to

Wait

(Henry Williamson, Stiffkey, Norfolk, 1938)

Out of the dark they speak, voices like owls',
the poets calling each to each again,
distinct yet coded: Thomas through the rain's
mesh, something akin to the wind howling
across the salt marsh, strangulated vowels
scarcely distinguishable though he strains
to separate the truth, the praise, the pain,
from nature's chaos where his last hope drowns.

Fasces and Eagles and the ruse of peace;
the politics too little and too late…
He lies all night beside his shotgun, wild-eyed,
begging old comrades for a quick release.
And death holds out the hand he once denied
until one cries from woods near Arras, *Wait!*

SH to JG from Williamson's Cottage, 2012

Provincials

So Petrarch lived here? First saw Laura here,
invented the sonnet and began a craze
that turned to 'tyranny'(your word). These days
they're hardly *de rigeur*, but there's the fear
that if you can't balance seven hundred years
on fourteen lines and five rhymes, then the Muse
will leave for Tony Harrison. There she goes.
But you and I have learned by now to steer
a steady course up Petrarch's mountain track
or – better metaphor – across the Rhône
beside that Pont that keeps on reaching for
a rhyme on its far bank. We know the knack
of picking a wind, too: not one that's blown
infernos; one that gently tries the door.

JG to SH from Avignon, 2012

a Post Card to

Castello

Primavera! The real first day of spring:
a lizard basking among the *semplici*.
In the *giardino de' Medici*
they have begun the slow uncovering
of the half-hardy orange trees, trimming
the box hedges' knotted geometry
back to a patient clipped formality.
And again in the bosco that blackbird singing...

On Monday, one by one, they'll start to bring
the potted lemons from the purgatory
of their winter home, their long dark reverie –
waiting as the dead await the living.
Then all the emergent buds will break expectantly,
dazed from their grotto, like Persephone.

SH to JG from Florence, 2013

a Post Card to

Librairie

Today a muse is playing games with me.
She follows in the shadows till I slip
out of the autumn sun into the bookshop
on the *Rue de la Parchminerie*.
And there she disappears beguilingly
among the shelves: I think I see her grip
a stack and bend and pull and squeeze her hips
into the section labelled *Poetry*.

A room, a secret space, hidden behind
the edifice of language by absurd
coincidence or irony, where she
the priestess of its sesame design
is free to come and go, to re-emerge
offering alternatives – or tea, or coffee.

SH to JG from Paris, 2014

a Post Card to

Megalith Mother

She opens up and, *oui, c'est vrai*, she is
the guardian of the dolmen, oh, it's been
three generations, *non*, her husband's gone
to work in Paris, he (the sunlight tries
to play on two horse chestnuts that disease
has rusted) he wants to sell, and no one's
interested now. Now, the standing stones,
their vast covering slabs, are all one sees
of any garden, where a climbing frame
or trampoline or swing might stand in other
more ordinary homes; so she is here
alone to care for this that's somehow come
down five thousand years to her, grey mother
of a dark into which we start to peer.

JG to SH from the Loire, 2016

a Post Card to

Sundial, San Petronius

A pinprick through the vaulted roof lets in
the simple light we live by, focused down
to one intense ellipse: miniature sun
that slides across the tesserae, creeping
towards an instant when it breaks the line
of days, weeks, months – a thin meridian
tracing its annual passage through the heavens
by each high-burnished, momentary noon.

And by that trail the old astronomers,
Cassini, Gugliemi, found that time
was fickle, slipshod, cheating as it passed:
hours lost by leap years on the calendar,
tomorrow, now and yesterday refined
exactly on their scale of shining brass.

SH to JG from Bologna, 2016

a Post Card to

Somersby

'root and all, and all in all'
     (Tennyson, 'Flower in the Crannied Wall')

A sonnet? Not out here. Even his wolds
are Kraken and Excalibur, revealing,
sinking back. Note, as you approach, a scowling
face, an outcrop, carved. Legends. Half-reaped fields.
An empty settle. There's a babbling child's
remembered brook. The font. A new-style calling
of kine in with a car-horn, their line filing
in search of its epic muse. She'll wait, holds

the six-bar gate, and sings. But, Tennyson –
whose house is just below, beside the grange
and opposite his father's tiny living –
do people love you still? High among crannies
on the crazed green sandstone church tower, strange,
that one perennial, bright yellow, thriving.

JG to SH from Lincolnshire, 2016

[41]

a Post Card to

From Aldeburgh

Sheer salt-bright light and a long shingle shore.
It drags your steps back as if the stones' pull
could sprawl you down and under like the rolled
grey waves that swell, smack, tumble and withdraw.
A place where not much grips: one pink crab claw,
seablite, horned poppies' blasted tentacles;
the fingers of a hundred shipwrecked souls
that cried out mercy in the breakers' roar.

Is it them you can hear in the backwash –
the pebbles chattering against the foam?
Raise up a shell and listen for that sound:
the wind, or Grimes' apprentices, the lost
girls huddled in the hulk *Ionia*…
high crowding voices that will not be drowned.

SH to JG, 2016
reverse: Maggi Hambling's Scallop

a Post Card to

August 8, 1829, Staffa

Ahead, the staves – so many times they've tolled
their one black note, but now a vivid stream
of beating sea-life breaks from Fingal's dream
and into Felix. No one cares. Not those cold
puking girls, not the eighty-two-year-old
who has a bucket list. We too would steam
towards that cubist portrait of a scream
wrapped in our own concerns. Someone is rolled
half witless, someone else is frying bacon
across the cello swell, the big tune, art
broken by nature. The romantic movement
moves on: its passengers look pale and shaken.
Except the one who's writing out a part
for wind, who thinks, yes, this is an improvement.

JG to SH from Hawthornden Castle, 2017

a Post Card to

Cranes Above Florence

They're always here, heads in the clouds
one foot in the Renaissance,
brooding like herons over the Arno,
each one a stilty miracle of steel geometry,
of mind over space and gravity.
The mercenaries of commerce
tend them and fly in them,
feed them as they might be a race
of gods; for as long as there's a city
men will require monuments, towers,
hive-cells, new stairs, new palaces…
So they're always here, turning
like mobiles, toiling to haul up
the perfect skyline – and spoiling it.

SH to JG, Florence, 2017

a Post Card to

(untitled)

So, what of Rome? City of monuments
pillars and obelisks, past upon past
one lain more heavily above the last –
Caesar and Emperor and Pope intent
on legacy, on showing what it meant
to conquer and to set your mark in vast
and desert lands, rich kingdoms east and west
and then to pass in pomp all passion spent.

They left us art and artefacts: an urn
a crypt, a column etched with hieroglyphs.
Though each in life was lauded in his turn
what they desired was honour without end.
Last (least?) the poets' water-written gifts;
Keats' fleeting spirit watched by Severn his friend.

SH to JG from Rome, 2017

a Post Card to

Last Post from Great Malvern

Through the mist it comes, dactylic beat
like the opening bars of *Cockaigne*, a bike
beginning to shape itself into handlebars
on an Edwardian face. Mr Phoebus
scrapes to a halt. His owner dismounts, approaches
the fluted, Doric pillar box, and wafts
a khaki package towards its embouchure.
A redcoat on sentry duty still,

now here it is on Twitter, the very same
Victorian postbox, as I'm about to post
a picture of me shaking hands with Elgar
(whose mother was a Greening) within the V
where Church Street meets Bellevue, at a dry
commemorative rock, the Enigma Fountain.

JG to SH from Great Malvern, 2018

a Post Card to

Giovanni di Paolo's *Flight into Egypt*

Three days of cloud then the sky clears: the sun
is up as we wake, gilding the hilltops
the east-facing slopes and the olive-tips
glistening below our window. It will soon
flatten its angles but for now the world shines
like a quattrocento painting, burnished
with hope, so even those two dull gossips
notice the flitting family. A sign?

Such things this morning resonate with us
though we live in an age of unbelief.
Let workmen stop today, gaze down the track
as long-cast shadows shorten in the dust –
to where the sunlight spreads like fine gold leaf
on Joseph's shoulders and the donkey's back.

SH to JG from Siena, 2018

a Post Card to

Keem

When a pleasant coast road suddenly uncoils
and rears hissing as if ready for attack,
it might seem wiser to have stayed in Böll's
retreat, and read accounts of how St Patrick
banished the snakes. But there is no retreating,
this nightmare doesn't even end at Keem –
there's only one way home. So now I'm waiting
for these sheep to count me back into their dream
of z-bend and sheer drop, in and out the cloud,
and down to sea-level. How their voices taunt me:
caar, yaaa, scaaared. And there's that cheery crowd
of geriatric pole-dancers. Avaunt ye,
white-haired weirdos. Ambition has to stop
its vaulting somewhere, like a coffee shop.

JG to SH from the Heinrich Böll Cottage,
Achill Island, 2018

a Post Card to

Another Silence

In Tuomiokirkko that September
the seventeen thousand came, Helsinki's
musicians played, while hand-picked minor keys
threw their mythologies open: a sombre
forest, a beating wing, a shore remembered
for some shift which might not even please
yet claims its fullness. Then finally he's
alone with an unknown opus number,
and we stand here today, while a maddening
tour group points and gestures excitedly
at nothing. I soon see why. They cannot speak,
they're deaf. If they have ever heard any
Sibelius, who knows. Yet their almighty
mute cry fills the church. We hear it rise and break.

JG to SH from Helsinki, 2019
reverse: Jean Sibelius at Ainola

a Post Card to

In Conwy Churchyard

Slow ivies grope across the tombs and twine
about the names of draper, shipwright, curate…
Their genealogies, set down in slate,
are safe now from the ravages of time.
Cut grass dries pale in the chisel's lines
and they serve too who only lie in wait
for Judgment that grows closer as the dates
slide backward into darkness like their lives.

But one plot sprouts sow-thistles where a nameless
child would sit and smile for the poet
who shaped for her a lasting kind of fame.
The Ballads' sentiments don't seem to fit
these days: her mound's caged with an iron grille.
Though spring's green yet, and they are seven still.

SH to JG from St Mary & All Saints Church,
Conwy, 2019

a Post Card to

Fountains

This afternoon's was trimmed with tortoises,
a witty touch. This morning's was the bold
Bernini one into which a horse's
rear end disappears. His giants lolled,
but high and dry at first – that little chap
had genitals to chlorinate before
the show could start. Then to a slow slip-slap
and gradual quenching of its urge to roar
the lion stoops and sips... Tonight, no doubt,
fresh neptunes, naiads, shells and waves, or just
a simple pipe emerging from the mouth
of some old Roman deity who's lost
for words, and spewing in a trough, will keep
things flowing, never still, and never deep.

JG to SH from Rome, 2019

a Post Card to

On a Theme from Marcus Aurelius

But what's the harm in hoping fame might come?
'It will distract you,' says Aurelius,
as Google magnifies him on his horse
in his own gallery. 'The gulf of time
before and after, not a trivial name,
is what you should consider.' Loud applause.
And so his name and fame come down to us,
insisting that a thumb is just a thumb
whichever way it turns, and though you're spent
and tangled in a gory net with bits
of cat and little hope but a mangled prayer,
while he's in laurelled white and gold up there,
hailed by the masses, one life's what he gets,
like yours, no more or less significant.

JG to SH from Rome, 2019

Postcard from Verona

Spirit of Juliet: leaves on the breeze
picked up and flirted down the ancient streets
where summer clings persistently to trees
that whisper quartos, folios of grief.
'There is no world without Verona's walls,'
they say, 'death is our end, loss is our sum.
No comfort keeps us when November's squalls
crowd howling in to mock the exiled sun.'
Yet year on year on year the lovers come
to make confession of their fears and dreams,
as if sheer human need made winter dumb
and what was sere and yellow spring with green.
Gleam then, desire, in their wishful eyes.
Love's tomb lies empty but hope never dies.

SH to JG, 2019

a Post Card to

Washing the Shopping

That time of year when I'd expect a card –
a poet's face, a castle, boats, hills, frescoes –
and you would too. Here in this yellowing yard,
there is no visiting, unless it's Tesco's.
A virtual greeting, then. What should it show?
The virus, like a seafront mine? Their graph
mountainscape? London empty? Or a rainbow
over clapping Cambridgeshire? The mask of grief
is quizzed by Zoom until it melts away,
and here two households partying athwart
each other's sofas (bunting, bubbly) raise
sly glasses as I pass. If I'd have caught
their moment... Instead (reverse) I appear
myself, washing the shopping. Wish you were here?

JG to SH, Stonely, Cambridgeshire, 2020

a Post Card to

Hilf dem Wald

Things take their time: the post, a book, a tree...
One card got lost in Italy for days
arriving home in retrospect (the ways
of track-and-trace were too arcane for me
to grasp) and yet when every family
is housebound, set apart, time lying lazy
on our hands, a rhyme like this can say
what can't be told by zooming instantly.

Remember too the wine from Germany,
a printed packet slipped around its neck
to *Hilf dem Wald?* An idea worth a try.
One seedling from the tray survived to stretch
up in the blue and flower seasonally,
five fathoms tall now, growing exponentially.

SH to JG, Catworth, Cambridgeshire, 2020

a Post Card to

From the Word-house

'Your well,
your way back down'
                    SH

It would decay, the Word-house, books and all
these drafts and notebooks, LPs, CDs, hard-drive
or software, if I didn't try to give
the boards a yearly coat of Cuprinol
to keep the weather off. No inch of wall,
yet this foxed sheet has managed to survive
my every clear-out – lines that somehow live
beyond their frame, in which you draw the well

outside my study, make of it a source,
a future 'way back down', as you here coin it
in free verse, fresh, unmoulded, from your Brickyard.
For home is where we most explore, of course,
when struggling through a thank-you note or sonnet.
It finds us, like an unexpected postcard.

JG to SH by hand, from Stonely

John Greening has received several major poetry prizes and a Cholmondeley Award. Since *Westerners* (1982) and *The Tutankhamun Variations* (1991), he has published over twenty collections, notably *To the War Poets* (Carcanet, 2013), *Heath* (Nine Arches, 2016, with Penelope Shuttle), and *The Silence* (Carcanet, 2019). His most recent publications are the sonnet sequence, *Europa's Flight* (New Walk, 2019), a group of music poems, *Moments Musicaux* (Salzburg Poetry, 2020), and a collection of his reviews: *Vapour Trails* (Shoestring, 2020). He has edited selections of Ian Crichton Smith and Geoffrey Grigson, and in 2015 produced a new edition of Edmund Blunden's *Undertones of War* for OUP. There has also been an Egypt memoir, *Threading a Dream*, and seven earlier books about poets and poetry. His anthologies include *Accompanied Voices: Poets on Composers, Ten Poems about Sheds* and the forthcoming *Hollow Palaces* (modern country house poems – with Kevin Gardner). He teaches for the Poetry School and was RLF Writing Fellow at Newnham College, Cambridge.

Stuart Henson received an Eric Gregory Award in 1979. Since then his poems and stories have appeared in a wide range of magazines and anthologies including *OxfordPoets* 2002, *Staying Alive* and *The Poetry Pharmacy*. His books include *The Impossible Jigsaw* and *Ember Music*, from Peterloo Poets, and *A Place Apart* and *The Odin Stone* from Shoestring Press. *The Way You Know It, New & Selected Poems*, was published by Shoestring in 2018. A new collection, *Beautiful Monsters*, is due in 2022.

Acknowledgements:

Acknowledgements are due to the editors and publishers of the magazines and books in which some of the poems originally appeared:

The Dark Horse, Manhattan Review (USA), *Metre, New Walk, The Spectator, Warwick Review, Wild Court, Write Where We Are Now* (Manchester Metropolitan University, 2020), *Fotheringhay and Other Poems* (Rockingham Press, 1995), *The Coastal Path* (Headland, 1996), *Nightflights* (Rockingham Press, 1998), *Iceland Spar* (Shoestring Press, 2008), *Hunts: Poems 1979–2009* (Greenwich Exchange, 2009), *Knot* (Worple Press, 2013), *Achill Island Tagebuch* (Redfoxpress, 2019) —JG

Agenda, The Dark Horse, Ember Music (Peterloo Poets, 1994), *Poems for Jeremy Corbyn* (Shoestring Press, 2016), *The Way You Know It* (Shoestring Press, 2018) —SH

A NOTE ON THE TYPES

The text typeface used in this book is Electra, designed by the
American type designer W. A. Dwiggins and first available from
Linotype in 1935. The name bears no relation to the Greek
character, but was adopted by Dwiggins to suggest
the 'crisp modernity' and 'electric' nature of his typeface,
independent as it was of historical models. The face
was digitized for electronic use in 1994.

Poem titles are in Avenir Light.